Table of Contents

A Field Guide for HR Leaders
Who Lead Quietly but Powerfully

The
POWER
of
PRESENCE

Elevating
HR Influence
Without the
Spotlight

Daphne B. Latimore

Paperback ISBN: 979-8-9995436-4-6
Hardback ISBN: 979-8-9995436-5-3

Published by

The Publishing Pad
www.thepublishingpad.com

Foreword

When I was called to transition my team to a business partner model, I knew exactly who I needed to contact: Daphne B. Latimore.

I had seen her work before—not just the results, but the way she worked. Daphne has a way of holding space that makes people stop, listen, and reconsider what they thought was possible. She doesn't just "advise." She influences the room with a calm clarity that redirects the energy and reframes the conversation.

One moment is still vivid in my memory where Daphne's prowess had a profound impact. At a leadership team meeting, as the conversation unfolded about setting the company calendar for the year, it became clear that HR was being cast—yet again—as the party planner and organizer. The default assumption was that we would own every company event on top of everything else on our plates.

Daphne didn't flinch. She didn't roll her eyes. She simply leaned in and said, "There are twelve of you here, each with large departments. I'm one person with a small team. We are not the party planners."

Her tone wasn't defensive. It was grounded. It was clear. And in that moment, the room shifted.

The silence was short, but it was powerful. You could see the realization wash over the group. That day, company activities became a shared responsibility—distributed evenly across departments, freeing HR to focus on the work that actually drives organizational impact.

That's what Daphne does. She doesn't just "show up." She reshapes the conversation so that HR's role is understood, respected, and leveraged for its strategic value.

This book, The Power of Presence, is not theory. It's Daphne's lived practice—refined through decades of leading, coaching, and partnering at the highest levels. As you read, you'll see how presence, when used with intention, becomes a force for both influence and integrity. You'll see how it redefines the role of HR, not as a function in the corner, but as a strategic driver at the center.

I'm honored to introduce you to her insights, and even more honored to call her a colleague and a thought partner.

—Mary-Beth, Senior HR Leader

INTRODUCTION

They Called Me "Stealth HR"

My boss once introduced me as his "stealth HR." When I asked what he meant, he said, "You do everything HR is supposed to do—shape culture, guide leaders, spot the genuine issues—but you do it without the red tape or the title. You make people better without making it about HR."

That comment changed how I viewed my work. It validated the influence I had built without always being visible or loud. It also reminded me that presence—not position—is what truly transforms HR leaders into strategic forces.

My influence hadn't come from being the loudest in the room or always stepping into the spotlight. In fact, it often came from knowing when to step in, what to illuminate, and how to elevate what mattered—especially when others weren't looking.

Presence is not about personal visibility. It's about directional clarity. It's the ability to focus the spotlight on the issues, patterns, people, and possibilities that drive real organizational change.

HR leadership doesn't always come with a stage, but it does come with responsibility. And when we embrace that, we lead not for applause, but for alignment.

That kind of presence isn't performative. It's practiced. It's built through intentionality—your energy, your timing, your ability to tune into both spoken and unspoken cues. It's the quiet assurance that comes not from needing the room's attention, but from knowing how to influence what happens in the room. Presence lives in how we listen, how we connect, and how we align people and performance in real time.

Presence wasn't something I stumbled into. It was something I built—moment by moment, meeting by meeting.

Like many HR professionals, I spent years sharpening my technical edge: employee relations, policy, talent strategy, compliance. I could execute flawlessly, but I didn't yet see myself as a people strategist. I was busy doing the work, not realizing I could shape the work.

At the time, the role I was stepping into didn't have a name. "Organizational strategist" wasn't part of the HR vocabulary—yet that's exactly what I was becoming. I wasn't just managing processes; I was influencing culture, aligning behavior with business goals, and guiding leaders through complexity.

That shift didn't happen overnight. Through experience, reflection, and a few well-timed teachable moments, I began to lead differently. I stopped simply responding to issues and started recognizing patterns. I stopped carrying the agenda and started shaping it. I began modeling the mindset and behaviors of an organizational strategist—connecting enterprise dots, elevating what mattered most, and stepping into my full influence.

On my last day in that corporate role, an employee stopped by to say goodbye. She smiled, and then quietly said, "Now who's going to look out for the people?" That simple question reminded me: the impact of presence isn't measured by visibility, but by the space you hold for others—even after you've left the room.

This book is a field guide for HR leaders ready to make that same shift. Not a traditional leadership manual or theoretical deep dive, but a practical, in-the-moment companion for those navigating the real dynamics of influence, trust, and credibility.

It's designed for HR leaders who know they bring more to the table than is often acknowledged, and who want to elevate their presence without losing authenticity. Whether you identify as quiet, bold, introverted, extroverted, seasoned, or emerging, your presence can become your power.

Like any trusted field guide, these pages offer frameworks, questions, and practices you can return to as the terrain changes. Because presence isn't a performance—it's a way of traveling through the work.

If you've ever asked yourself:

- How do I increase my influence without chasing visibility?
- How do I get my voice heard at the table without having to prove my worth over and over?
- How do I lead culture, not just manage compliance?

. . . then this book is for you.

We're going beyond posture and polish. We're getting into mind-set, modeling, and mission. Because presence isn't something you perform. It's something you practice, and, ultimately, something you embody.

Let's begin.

PART I
Understanding Presence

Presence isn't about being the loudest voice in the room—it's about being the clearest signal in the noise.

Before we can practice presence, we must first understand it. In today's workplace, where attention is scarce and trust is earned moment by moment, the concept of "presence" is often misunderstood as charisma, extroversion, or stage-commanding confidence. But presence—especially for HR professionals and strategic leaders—isn't about performance. It's about alignment.

Part I lays the foundation by answering a central question: What is presence, really?

We explore it as more than posture or polish. We examine it as a leadership stance—one that is internal before it is ever external. These chapters challenge you to consider how your thoughts, values, and energy influence how you show up in conversations, decisions, and organizational culture.

Through reflection prompts, practice tips and alignment challenges, this section helps you reconnect with the essence of presence: being fully engaged, authentic, and intentional in every interaction. Whether you're navigating change, advocating for people, or influencing at the executive table, your presence shapes how your leadership is received—and remembered.

This part is not about changing who you are. It's about uncovering the influence of your presence—grounded in authenticity, clarity, and connection—and learning how to bring it forward with confidence and purpose.

Let's begin with understanding the presence you already carry, and the potential it holds.

CHAPTER 1

Presence Is Not a Performance

HR is often misunderstood. It's seen as the department that plans birthday celebrations, manages annual reviews, or shows up only when something goes wrong. Because of this, many HR leaders unconsciously adopt the mindset of a performer. We smile through burnout, mediate with neutrality, and work behind the scenes—thinking the more invisible we are, the better.

In my earliest years in HR, I believed my success was tied to likability. If I could fix problems quickly, quietly, and with a smile, people would like me—and if they liked me, I reasoned, they would trust me. If I stayed agreeable and helpful, I would be seen as essential. But I learned the hard way that people-pleasing is not the key to influence. I needed to cultivate **presence**—an air of authority that leads to influence.

So, how is presence achieved?

There's a long-standing myth in leadership circles that presence is a performance—that if you want to be seen as credible, competent, and capable, you need to project these traits through big energy, bold talk, and assertive confidence. For HR professionals, this belief often results in pressure to show up in ways that don't feel authentic—or, worse, a feeling that we should stay silent if we don't fit that mold.

But let's be clear: Presence is not a performance. It's not something you put on like a costume when it's time to impress a room. It's not about being charismatic, extroverted, or the loudest voice in a meeting.

Presence is something deeper. It's rooted in clarity, consistency, and connection. It's about:

- Knowing your purpose in a room
- Bringing awareness to how your energy influences others
- Listening before speaking
- Speaking with intention, not for attention
- Holding space—not dominating it

When HR leaders treat presence as a performance, they burn themselves out trying to "prove" their value in every meeting. They overcompensate, become overly agreeable, or avoid speaking up unless they have crafted the perfect statement. This kind of performance-based presence is exhausting, and ultimately ineffective.

True presence is sustainable. It allows you to:

- Be fully engaged, even when you're not speaking
- Influence decisions through questions, not just answers
- Offer quiet authority that resonates long after the meeting ends

But to even reach that level of presence, we must confront one of the biggest myths about our profession: Everyone believes they can do HR.

People assume HR is about being friendly, likable, and keeping people happy. They believe it's rooted in pleasantries and policies—not in strategy, systems, or organizational dynamics.

Here's the truth: HR is not about pleasing people. It's about aligning people. It's about making tough decisions, facilitating healthy tension, and advocating for the long game when everyone else is focused on the now.

The myth persists because real HR—strategic HR—is often invisible. When done well, it looks seamless. But behind the scenes, it requires:

- Reading unspoken dynamics in the room
- Helping leaders face uncomfortable truths
- Navigating ambiguity with empathy and resolve
- Balancing business objectives with human needs

Defining Presence

Presence isn't about charisma or popularity. It's not about having all the answers. Presence is the energy you bring into a space—the way you hold your seat at the table, not for status, but for stewardship. It's the ability to be fully engaged, emotionally available, and attuned to others in the moment, without distraction, judgment, or the need to perform.

Presence isn't about taking up space; it's about making space. It is a form of influence—not through authority, but through authenticity, focus, and connection. Presence transforms conversations, deepens relationships, and shapes culture.

Real presence is when you're able to:

- Speak a difficult truth with grace
- Hold silence with confidence
- Ask questions that change the direction of a conversation
- Stay grounded when others react emotionally

When you stop performing and start practicing presence, you lead with credibility—not just comfort.

Presence, in this context, becomes a form of leadership. It's how you show up when no one is watching. It's the tone you set even before you speak. And it's the strategic choice to lead with alignment, not approval.

When I Stopped Performing

I'll never forget a defining moment early in my director-level role. A senior leader praised me in a meeting for "keeping the peace" during a contentious organizational change. Later, a peer pulled me aside and said, "You're great at smoothing things over but I didn't actually hear your perspective."

That comment landed like a gut punch. I realized I had become an expert at making others comfortable but I wasn't contributing with intention. I was facilitating harmony instead of leading strategically.

Presence is about standing rooted in clarity—not simply seeking harmony. It's about voicing difficult truths with integrity, not diluting them for comfort. It's about creating space for meaning, not rushing to fill silence with words.

REFLECTION:
Where Are You Performing?

- In which situations at work do you find yourself "putting on" a version of presence?
- Where do you feel the most aligned, grounded, and authentic?

PRESENCE PRACTICE

In your next meeting, choose to speak last. Listen fully. When you do speak, anchor your point to values or outcomes—not reactions.

ALIGNMENT CHALLENGE
Review a recent decision or interaction. Did your presence help shape the direction, or did you simply adapt to others' expectations?

Throughout this book, we'll explore how presence shapes perception, how perception shapes influence, and how influence shapes outcomes. But it starts here—with this truth: You don't have to perform to lead. You have to be present to lead.

CHAPTER 2

The Anatomy of HR Presence

In chapter 1, we briefly talked about presence but what is presence—really?

It's a word we hear often in leadership circles, but it's rarely defined in a way that feels actionable, especially for HR professionals. Presence isn't just about how you carry yourself. It's about how your presence carries meaning for others.

In HR, our presence has the ability to stabilize, to shift, and to transform—not because we control the room, but because we center it.

Presence, through our lens, is the intentional alignment of awareness, energy, and influence—used to create clarity, connection, and confidence in others.

It's not an act. It's not a title. It's a state of being that invites trust and builds credibility over time. It's what allows you to:

- Read the room without losing yourself in it.
- Hold tension without absorbing the chaos.

- Speak truth without needing the spotlight.
- Represent people without making it personal.

Let's break it down.

More Than a First Impression

We've all heard the phrase *executive presence*. It often conjures up images of a polished speaker, a strong handshake, or someone who can command a room with few words. But for HR leaders—especially those operating at the intersection of people and power—presence must be deeper than posture and polish.

Presence is not just how others see you. It's how you see yourself, how you engage with others, and how you move through complexity with intentionality.

In my own evolution as an HR leader, I realized that presence wasn't just about what I said in the room. It was also about how I prepared before I entered, how I responded when tensions rose, and how I aligned my behavior with my values. That's when I began to understand presence not as a single trait, but as a multilayered system of capabilities that can be practiced and refined.

The Foundation: Inner Presence

Let's begin with what lies beneath the surface, the internal anatomy that supports all visible expressions of presence. Inner presence is built on four elements:

1. Awareness

Awareness must come first: awareness of self, of others, and of the broader system you're operating within. It's emotional intelligence with an enterprise lens.

Awareness includes:

- Knowing your own triggers and tendencies.
- Reading group energy and subtle dynamics.
- Understanding the timing and readiness for action.

2. Alignment

This is where intention meets behavior. Alignment is about congruence—ensuring that how you show up matches what you stand for. When your body language, tone, and choices align with your role as a strategic leader, people trust you. Alignment isn't perfection. It's integrity in motion.

3. Advocacy

Presence is not passive. It includes the courage to advocate for what matters, even when it's uncomfortable. For HR professionals, that means elevating the people lens in every decision, naming misalignments, and championing both performance and well-being.

4. Accountability

True presence holds weight. It doesn't seek to be right; it seeks to be responsible. Accountability is being mindful of your impact, following through on commitments, and holding others accountable with compassion and clarity.

The Outer Expression:
Visible Presence

Once you've cultivated inner presence, it begins to shape your outer presence—how others experience you: what they see, hear, and feel when you enter the room. Outer presence is expressed through four dimensions that influence conversations, decisions, and culture:

1. Precision

Precision is the discipline of speaking with clarity and intention. It's the ability to cut through noise and name what matters most, so others can act with confidence. Leaders with precision don't just share information—they focus it in a way that moves the room forward.

Example: "We've discussed engagement, but what I'm observing is withdrawal. That's where we need to focus."

2. Resonance

Resonance is a connection that lasts beyond the moment. It's the ability to communicate in a way that is remembered, quoted, and acted upon, because it aligns with both logic and emotion. Resonance happens when people feel both understood and inspired to respond.

Example: After a difficult restructuring, you follow up with, "I want to acknowledge the weight of this decision and explore how we can rebuild together."

3. Anchor

Anchor is presence under pressure. It's the steadiness you bring when others feel uncertain or overwhelmed. Leaders who anchor offer structure without rigidity—providing a clear path forward while holding space for complexity.

Example: "There are three layers to what we're facing. Let's address the one that will create the most momentum today."

4. Imprint

Imprint is the lasting effect of your contribution—the insight, trust, or clarity you leave behind long after the conversation ends. It's not about being the loudest voice; it's about offering something that shifts perspective or direction in meaningful ways.

Example: Weeks later, a colleague cites your insight to reframe a strategy discussion.

Bridging Inner Presence and Visible Presence

Inner presence is the quiet agreement between your values and your behavior. Outer presence is how others experience that agreement in action.

The most powerful HR leaders I've worked with are masters of both. They cultivate self-awareness and alignment, and then they express it through precision, resonance, anchor, and imprint. Their presence isn't an act; it's an extension of their integrity.

REFLECTION:
What Is Your Presence Rooted In?

- Do you know what it feels like when you're fully aligned?
- When was the last time someone responded to your presence without you having to say much?

PRESENCE PRACTICE

- Observe your energy for a full day. Are you reactive or responsive? Anchored or adapting to every voice in the room?
- Ask a trusted colleague: "How would you describe my presence in meetings?" Then listen—without explanation.

ALIGNMENT CHALLENGE

Choose one of the four pillars—Awareness, Alignment, Advocacy, or Accountability—and make it your focus for the week. How does your presence shift when you lead with that intention?

The four elements of inner presence—awareness, alignment, advocacy, and accountability—form the foundation of presence. You'll see them throughout this book, shaping how HR leaders build influence, increase credibility, and lead boldly without shouting.

But presence doesn't stop there. It also lives in how others experience us—in the precision of our message, the resonance of our relationships, the anchor we bring in moments of pressure, and the imprint our actions leave long after we've left the room. Presence is not a switch you flip. It's a muscle you build.

And when practiced consistently, presence becomes more than how you show up—it becomes how you shape the space around you.

In the next chapter, we'll explore why building credibility is more powerful than chasing visibility, and how presence helps you do both without sacrificing authenticity.

CHAPTER 3

Credibility Before Visibility

There's a tension many HR leaders feel but rarely name: the need to be seen versus the need to be trusted.

The Visibility Trap

HR leaders have long been encouraged to "earn a seat at the table"—to be present in strategy meetings, to demonstrate our value through visibility. And we've risen to the challenge: showing up on task forces, leading town halls, partnering with leadership teams. We show up fully, hoping not just to be seen, but to be trusted.

But presence is not performance. And visibility, without the weight of credibility, can be fleeting. It gets noticed, but not always valued.

I've worked alongside brilliant HR professionals whose insight could shape strategy, culture, and outcomes. Yet too often, they find themselves present but not heard. Their expertise acknowledged, but not acted upon. It's not a reflection of their capability; it's a signal that presence must carry not just visibility, but voice and influence.

What's missing isn't effort. It's strategic alignment. And when presence is rooted in credibility, the conversation shifts.

The Teachable Moment That Shifted Me

I remember sitting in an executive leadership meeting during a period of significant restructuring. The conversation turned, predictably, toward workforce reductions. I had come prepared—data, engagement risks, insights on morale. As the conversation intensified, I took a deliberate pause, listening for the currents underneath the discussion. I was gauging where the decision-makers were leaning and when my input would have the greatest impact. But as the meeting moved quickly toward resolution, I realized that the right moment for influence doesn't always announce itself. Sometimes, you have to create it.

After the meeting, our CFO pulled me aside. "Daphne," he said, "you bring strong business acumen. You engage fully with the team. But when it comes to HR matters, you seemed less energized today."

Then he added something I'll never forget:

"We don't just count on you to support decisions—we count on you to shape them. You help us align and lead the workforce. That's the difference you bring."

It wasn't a rebuke. It was a reminder—a signal of trust.

They weren't looking for me to show up quietly. They were relying on me to lead visibly, credibly, and with full presence.

That conversation shifted something foundational.

It was the moment I stopped trying to validate my seat at the table, and started owning the value I was there to bring. Not through volume, but through voice. Not through visibility, but through presence.

What Credibility Looks Like in Practice

Credibility is earned when:

- Your insights change how leaders make decisions.
- Your absence is felt as much as your presence.
- People say, "I didn't like what they said, but I needed to hear it."

In the eyes of your peers and senior leaders, credibility isn't about charm or visibility, it's about:

- Clarity under pressure.
- Courage in complexity.
- Consistency over time.
- Contributions that move the business forward.

It's the silent vote of confidence that says: This person isn't just in the room. This person shapes the room.

A Tale of Two HR Leaders

Let me show you what this looks like through two professionals I've coached—names changed for privacy:

Maya had all the energy of a rising star. She volunteered for every committee, posted regularly on the company intranet, and was highly visible to leadership. But her insights were often reactive. She over-relied on popularity with peers and hesitated to push back when her recommendations were challenged.

Elena, on the other hand, rarely spoke in meetings. But when she spoke, leaders listened. Her contributions were sharp, people-centered, and aligned to business strategy. She'd often anticipate executive concerns and bring data to the table before anyone asked. Eventually, her role expanded beyond HR, because her credibility transcended her function.

Maya had visibility but not traction. Elena had traction; then visibility followed.

The difference? Presence rooted in credibility.

What Business Leaders Really Want

In conversations with CEOs, COOs, and CFOs over the years, I've seen one theme emerge: They don't want HR leaders who simply "manage people issues." They want thought partners who see around corners.

They value:

- HR leaders who connect people data to business risk.
- Partners who name tensions early and help resolve them quietly.
- Voices that bring behavioral insight into financial decisions.

When you bring clarity, advocacy, and accountability to your conversations with senior management—when you consistently align your intention with your presence—you don't have to fight for influence. You become influential.

Anchoring Presence: Your Credibility Quotient

Think of credibility as your invisible equity. You build it with every follow-through, every insight that resonates, every moment you hold steady while others react.

And, just like financial equity, credibility compounds.

So ask yourself: Are you investing in your credibility? Or just collecting receipts of visibility?

REFLECTION:
Beyond the Spotlight—Credibility as Currency

- Where are you most tempted to chase visibility over depth?
- What would shift if you prioritized building credibility—even if it meant fewer spotlights?

PRESENCE PRACTICE

Before your next senior meeting:

- Prepare one insight that connects employee behavior to business outcomes.
- Anticipate one unspoken concern, and be ready to offer a solution.

ALIGNMENT CHALLENGE

Audit your "credibility equity" with key stakeholders:

- Who consistently trusts your judgment?
- Who listens but doesn't act?
- Who doesn't yet see your value?

Choose one relationship to strengthen—not through more meetings, but through meaningful contribution that anticipates business needs and aligns with your presence.

PART II

The Strategic Shift

Presence becomes incredibly powerful when it evolves from personal posture to organizational influence.

In this section, we move beyond foundational awareness and begin exploring how presence transforms our role—from functional executors to strategic leaders. This is the shift that defines the future of HR.

Where Part I focused on how you show up, Part II explores what happens when you lead differently. It's about moving from reactive problem-solving to proactive sense-making. From enforcing policies to interpreting culture. From observing decisions to shaping them.

Each chapter in Part II will unpack how presence fuels:

- Strategic insight
- Real-time influence
- Systems-level coaching
- The ability to lead cultural momentum—not just manage it

This is the moment where presence becomes leverage.

Because when HR leads with intention, pattern recognition, and enterprise awareness, we stop waiting for permission, and start transforming outcomes.

CHAPTER 4

From Policy to Pattern Recognition

Traditional HR has long been associated with rules, policies, and compliance. These elements are essential—they ensure equity, mitigate risk, and provide the consistency organizations need. But they are not enough. Presence calls us to engage beyond enforcement—to interpret what's happening beneath the surface and shape what's possible.

Policies set expectations, but they don't change culture. Compliance reduces liability, but it doesn't build leadership capacity.

As HR leaders elevate their presence, one of the most powerful shifts they can make is moving from being policy enforcers to pattern recognizers.

From Rules to Relevance

Pattern recognition is where relevance begins. It's a strategic capability rooted in presence. Instead of asking, "What rule was broken?" HR leaders ask, "What is this behavior telling us about how we operate, lead, and relate?"

This shift transforms HR from compliance enforcer to culture strategist. When you develop the capacity to recognize and interpret patterns, you begin to:

- Anticipate disruption before it surfaces as conflict or disengagement.
- Address root causes, not just surface-level symptoms.
- Influence systems, not just intervene in moments.

A single complaint may point to an individual concern. But three complaints across departments about transparency? That's not a coincidence—it's a cultural cue.

Pattern recognition connects dots across behavior, communication, and leadership. It turns isolated feedback into strategic insight. When you respond from that place of presence, you're not just solving problems—you're shaping the system that created them.

A Real Moment of Shift

Years ago, I worked with a leadership team where conflict and burnout were on the rise. Employees were increasingly disengaged, and the formal complaints were mounting. On paper, each issue looked different—interpersonal disputes, vague role expectations, missed deadlines. The instinct was to address them case-by-case, to "clean up the mess."

But something didn't sit right. As I sat in listening sessions and reviewed the language in exit interviews, a pattern emerged: people didn't feel safe to be honest. Feedback was filtered. Decisions were made behind closed doors. The significant issues weren't procedural—they were relational and cultural.

The solution wasn't a new policy or a better escalation protocol. It was creating a manager development program that taught how to deliver feedback, build trust, and facilitate psychological safety because those were the root causes beneath the noise.

Pattern recognition isn't about collecting data. It's about interpreting human systems in real time. It shifts HR from passive observation to active insight, enabling leaders to connect behavior to culture and action to meaning.

Presence as a Pattern Tool

Pattern recognition requires presence. It means:

- Listening actively.
- Noticing subtle shifts in tone and behavior.
- Tracking repetition in conversations.
- Asking questions that uncover meaning rather than just managing risk.

For presence to be useful as a pattern tool, you must be willing to speak to what you see, even when it's uncomfortable.

This is where credibility and presence intersect: Do people trust you enough to name what's unspoken? Can you elevate patterns without creating defensiveness? Can you translate tension into transformation?

From Insight to Influence

The ultimate goal is not to gather more information—it's to convert insight into influence.

That influence can take many forms:

- Reframing a leadership development program based on engagement trends
- Introducing a new communication cadence after noticing siloed thinking
- Advising on restructure strategy by identifying invisible decision-making patterns

When you lead with presence, your insights land differently. They are not just observations—they're doorways into systemic change.

REFLECTION:
Where Are the Patterns?

- What recurring issues do you see across teams or departments?
- Are there disconnects between what leaders say and how they behave?
- Where do surface-level issues point to deeper cultural gaps?

PRESENCE PRACTICE

For one week:

- Track informal feedback and emotional undercurrents during meetings
- Listen closely to what's repeated, and what's avoided

Ask yourself: "What's the broader signal here?" Then bring one of those patterns into conversation—with curiosity, not criticism.

ALIGNMENT CHALLENGE

Choose one issue you've historically addressed with a policy or directive.

Reframe it through the lens of pattern recognition: identify the system, belief, or behavior beneath the issue.

Instead of drafting a new rule, propose a solution that addresses the root of the issue.

CHAPTER 5

The Language of Influence

Presence without communication is invisible.

Influence without language is lost.

You can have the deepest insight in the room, but if you can't articulate it clearly and strategically, it won't land. The most credible leaders aren't just heard; they're understood. They speak truth in ways that prompt action, not just agreement.

That's why the most effective HR professionals are not just policy stewards or people experts; they're fluent translators. They speak the languages of operations, finance, strategy, and culture—and they facilitate communication among them without losing the integrity of the employee experience. They are the champions of the employee value proposition, ensuring that what the organization promises is reflected in what employees actually experience.

Becoming Bilingual: Head and Heart

Strategic HR leaders are bilingual—not in a linguistic sense, but in the way they connect:

- Business priorities with human realities
- Data with dialogue
- Structure with story
- Accountability with dignity

This is presence in action—stepping in as someone who bridges what is often divided. You become a trusted interpreter, helping leaders see the impact of their choices and helping employees understand the context behind decisions.

And because your language is grounded in both logic and care, your influence leaves an imprint. You're not just heard—you're believed.

A Defining Conversation

Early in my executive journey, I began to see that presenting data wasn't enough—leaders needed me to help them connect the dots. One day, I was in a senior leadership meeting, sharing turnover data. I had my charts, my retention rates, my comparison points. I framed it as "a concern we needed to keep an eye on." After the meeting, a leader pulled me aside and said, "Daphne, that data was helpful, but it didn't move me. What does it mean for how we operate? What risk does this create?"

They weren't asking me for more numbers; they were asking me for meaning. They needed me to interpret what I was seeing, to draw the line from data to decision, and to help them see what was at stake. That moment crystallized for me that my leaders didn't just need me to represent the data—they needed me to illuminate its meaning and guide them toward the decisions that would shape our future.

From that point on, I reframed my communication:

- "Here's what we're seeing on the ground."
- "Here's how it affects your KPIs and timelines."
- "Here's the risk of inaction, and the opportunity if we lead differently."
- Most importantly: **"Here's how we solve it—together."**

Influence Happens in Framing

You don't need to say more to be more influential. You need to say what matters—clearly, courageously, and in a way others can act on.

The language of influence sounds like:

- "What this means for the business is . . ."
- "If this behavior continues, here's the likely impact . . ."
- "The opportunity here is to align people strategy with the proposed initiative . . ."
- "We're not just seeing resistance; we're seeing confusion that needs clarity."

It's not about sounding impressive. It's about being relevant and responsible with your words.

Language Shifts that Build Presence

How we say things is just as important as what we say. These subtle but powerful shifts in language help HR leaders translate insight into influence, turning observations into action and increasing the credibility of their presence.

1. Strategic Framing

Instead of: "We're launching a new engagement survey."

Say: "We're collecting insights to identify what's driving team performance and retention."

2. Behavior-Based Language

Talk in terms of behavior rather than personality.

Instead of: "The manager is difficult."

Say: "The manager frequently interrupts team members, which is impacting trust and participation."

3. Clear Connection to Business Value

Talk in terms of a clear connection to business value rather than merely offering commentary.

Instead of: "There's low morale."

Say: "We're seeing avoidance behaviors, slower decision-making, and decreased cross-team collaboration."

These three shifts in language will make your observations more useful, and your presence more credible.

Language as Leadership Presence

When your language reflects your strategic understanding, your presence is amplified. People don't just hear what you say; they trust that you've thought it through. That you see the whole picture. That you're not speaking from reaction, but from reflection.

In this way, presence becomes a leadership multiplier. It transforms every conversation, every recommendation, every pause before you speak into a moment of alignment and influence.

REFLECTION:
How Do You Frame Your Insight?

- Do you lead with HR language or business language?
- How often do you tie your recommendations to enterprise risk or opportunity?
- Are your insights designed to inform or to activate?

PRESENCE PRACTICE

In your next meeting:

- Use this structure:

    » Here's what I'm observing:
    » Here's what it means for the business:
    » Here's what I recommend we do about it:

- Replace at least one abstract phrase with a behavior-based observation. For example, "Team morale is low" might become "We've seen a 30% drop in meeting participation over the last sixty days."

ALIGNMENT CHALLENGE

Choose a recent HR memo, talking point, or meeting contribution and rewrite it using one of the three language shifts described in this chapter:

- Strategic Framing
- Behavior-Based Language
- Connection to Business Value

Then share the rewrite with a peer or mentor and ask: "Does this help you act faster or think differently?" You may take it a step forward by sharing both the original and the rewrite for comparison from the reader's perspective.

When your language brings clarity, invites action, and reflects intention, you don't just influence—you lead. Because when presence is expressed through purposeful communication, it becomes visible, credible, and indispensable. When your language sharpens decision-making, your presence becomes indispensable.

CHAPTER 6

Showing Up in the Rooms That Matter

"I wasn't on the invite list, but I asked to observe the strategy session. Halfway through, someone turned to me and said, 'What's your take?' That moment changed how I saw my role, and how they saw me."
—HR Generalist

Presence doesn't begin and end in HR meetings.

It doesn't stop at your department's goals or your calendar's comfort zone. If you want to lead strategically, you need to show up where strategy is being shaped: in operations, finance, innovation, compliance, and the boardroom.

Because those rooms are not only where decisions are made. They are where priorities are set, risks are balanced, and trade-offs are negotiated.

And, too often, the people lens enters the conversation after the fact—when morale dips, turnover spikes, or burnout becomes a headline.

Sometimes HR isn't invited into those rooms.

Other times, we're there—but silent.

The Risk of Silence

There are many reasons we might stay silent. We tell ourselves we're still learning the business. Or that our insights might slow things down. Or that it's "not the right moment" to speak up.

But here's the truth: presence without participation is passive, and passive presence doesn't move strategy.

Being in the room is step one.

Helping shape the conversation is step two.

Strategic presence is more than being articulate or confident. It's the ability to influence outcomes by aligning your insight, language, and behavior to the moment at hand. It means bringing not just expertise, but intention: reading the room, understanding what's at stake, and offering perspective that advances the conversation, not just fills the air. If we are truly to be stewards of the workforce and culture, we must stop waiting for permission to contribute. We must walk in with clarity, curiosity, and a point of view grounded in insight.

What Strategic Presence Looks Like in Action

Strategic presence isn't about volume—it's about value. It's the ability to show up with purpose, clarity, and confidence, as a thought partner who helps move the conversation forward. It means:

- Building trust with decision-makers before the meeting begins.
- Understanding the business drivers well enough to connect them to human capability.
- Speaking up when behavior and strategy are misaligned, even if you're the lone dissenting voice.

Strategic presence doesn't require you to take over the room.

It invites you to elevate the conversation. It means tilting the lens just enough so that people, behavior, and sustainability are not afterthoughts—they're inputs.

I've seen HR leaders add tremendous value just by asking:

- "What do we want people to experience during this change?"
- "Have we accounted for the feedback loops we'll need to sustain this shift?"
- "What might be the unintended consequences on front-line teams?"

These aren't soft questions. They're strategic interventions.

The Credibility Continuum

To show up credibly in these rooms, you don't have to know every financial metric or regulatory code. But you do need to understand the levers that drive the business. You need to connect the dots between organizational health and business performance, and communicate those connections fluently.

You earn that seat over time by:

- Being consistent
- Bringing forward relevant insights
- Avoiding defensiveness
- Always grounding your contributions in shared enterprise goals

Credibility earns you presence.

But contribution sustains it.

A Story from the Table

In one organization, I was invited to a leadership team meeting that had nothing to do with HR—at least on paper. It was about expanding a product line and evaluating supplier relationships. I listened. I asked a single question: "How will this expansion impact the workload distribution across our regional teams?"

The room went quiet. No one had considered that yet.

That moment sparked a deeper dive into operations and workforce readiness, which ultimately saved the company six figures in rework and turnover.

Presence isn't always about having the answer.

It's about asking the question no one else thought to ask.

REFLECTION:
Are You in the Right Rooms?

- What key decisions are being made without your insight?
- Where are you holding back—not because you're unqualified, but because you're uncertain of your value?
- What's one room you should be in but aren't (yet)?

PRESENCE PRACTICE

- Ask to sit in on a cross-functional or executive team meeting as an observer.
- Beforehand, identify two areas where HR could elevate the discussion, and prepare one insight or question that brings a people-centric lens into the room.

ALIGNMENT CHALLENGE

- Identify one strategic forum where your presence would create value, whether that's a leadership huddle, budget review, innovation sprint, or board subcommittee.
- Begin building the relationships, business fluency, and credibility to earn and maximize that seat.

When you walk into a room that matters, don't just take up space—embody your presence. Let your inner clarity, courage, and accountability shape the way you anchor the conversation. Let your precision, resonance, and imprint turn the room into a place where meaning is made and direction is set. That's how you don't just join the room—you define it.

PART III

Practicing the Presence

Presence isn't just something you understand. It's something you practice.

You've built the awareness. You've shifted your strategy. Now, the question becomes:

How do you sustain presence in the complexity of real leadership? This part of the book is where theory meets tension. Where values meet resistance. Where your influence is evaluated not in perfect moments, but in pressured ones.

You'll explore what it means to lead before you speak, to influence from the shadows, and to stand grounded when stakes are high. These are the moments that define not just how you're seen, but what kind of culture follows your lead.

CHAPTER 7

Model the Mindset Before the Message

"Before delivering layoffs, I centered myself: deep breath, value check, clear message. One person said, 'I could tell you cared, even before you spoke.' That's when I understood the power of mindset."
—HR Director

Presence doesn't start with your words. It starts with your orientation—the inner stance you take before you ever open your mouth.

Too often, we prepare for critical conversations by crafting the message. We obsess over tone, talking points, timing. But people don't just hear what we say. They feel how we show up.

When your mindset is reactive, defensive, or performative, no amount of polish will mask it.

When your mindset is grounded, intentional, and aligned, your message lands, even if it's hard to hear.

The Inner Signal

I once coached an HR leader who had to deliver difficult feedback to a COO. She came in with her data, her documentation, and her script. But her energy was tight. She was bracing for battle.

And sure enough, the message fell flat.

We paused and recalibrated. I asked her, "What would it look like to approach this as a partner, not a protector?"

In their next meeting, her tone shifted. Her posture softened. She led with shared outcomes, not accusation. And the conversation opened.

Mindset creates space. Message delivers insight.

Presence delivers both.

Three Anchoring Questions Before You Speak

1. What's my intention? Not just what I want to say, but what do I want to create with this message?
2. What energy am I bringing into this space? Am I reactive? Defensive? Clear? Curious?
3. What does the room need from me right now?

Sometimes presence means pausing. Other times, it means disrupting.

REFLECTION:
What Drives Your Message?

- Do you prepare for meetings by rehearsing your words—or grounding your mindset?
- When have you noticed a mismatch between how you intended a statement or action and how it was received?

PRESENCE PRACTICE

Before your next difficult conversation:

- Pause and check your orientation.
- Write your intention, not just your agenda.
- Focus less on saying it right, and more on *being* right (that is, aligned).

ALIGNMENT CHALLENGE

- Think of a recent message that didn't land. Revisit your mindset at the time. What would you shift now?
- Rehearse that message again—with presence as your starting point.

Presence isn't something you layer on after the fact. It begins with how you see yourself in the room, and what you believe your role is in the conversation. When you model the mindset before the message, you don't just deliver information; you create conditions for understanding, trust, and forward movement. In a world overloaded with noise, presence becomes your signal. Make it intentional.

CHAPTER 8

Leading in the Margins— The Art of Stealth HR

At the start of this book, I mentioned a moment I was referred to as "stealth HR."

What I've come to realize is that I wasn't alone.

Stealth HR exists everywhere.

It's the HR business partner who shifts hiring strategy without making a formal announcement.

It's the advisor who introduces a leadership lens so subtly that others claim it as their own.

It's the coach who shifts culture one sidebar at a time.

Stealth HR is not about hiding. It's about harnessing influence in its most strategic form: subtle, intentional, and transformative.

Beyond the Spotlight

In the age of performance reviews, leadership scorecards, and culture dashboards, we've grown accustomed to the idea that HR's impact must be measurable—and visible.

But not every transformation announces itself.

Some of the most effective changes happen in the margins:

- A shift in how a leader speaks to their team
- A new norm quietly adopted across departments
- A toxic behavior that disappears without a memo

These outcomes don't require applause. They require presence.

A Framework for Stealth HR

Stealth HR follows a pattern—one that allows leaders to operate with care, strategy, and impact. I call it **the OSIE Model**:

1. Observe
Start by watching as dynamics unfold. Notice where power resides, how conflict shows up, and what's not being said.

2. Seed
Plant insights in ways that don't create resistance. Ask questions. Introduce language. Offer perspective without ownership.

3. Influence

Support others as they carry the message forward. Help leaders believe the insight came from within the team. You don't need credit—you need alignment.

4. Exit

Let go once the shift is underway. Don't hover. Let the system own the change. Let the behavior—not your title—carry the impact forward.

This is influence without ego. And it works.

CASE STUDY 1:
The Conflict That Disappeared

A senior leader had become the center of low morale—frequent miscommunication, public microaggressions, and increasing turnover. But the team's numbers looked strong. The CEO didn't see a reason to act.

Instead of forcing the issue, I requested to facilitate their next team retreat. I built a debrief exercise that surfaced themes without naming names. It gave the team language. It gave the leader insight.

Within weeks, one-on-one conversations began. Coaching was requested. By quarter-end, feedback loops were in place and the conflict behaviors had shifted.

There was no investigation. No formal reprimand. Just pattern recognition, behavioral visibility, and accountability—seeded strategically.

CASE STUDY 2:
A Culture Reframe

At another company, DEI efforts were stalling. Executives wanted to "rebrand" the initiative. Instead of debating definitions, I invited cross-functional leaders to share what inclusion looked like in their departments.

We didn't publish a new DEI statement. We crowdsourced stories. We curated examples. We let the behaviors build the brand.

Months later, those same executives referenced the language from those sessions—adopting it as the new cultural standard.

Stealth HR doesn't fight to be heard. It listens deeply and shifts the current.

When to Employ Stealth, and When Not To

Stealth HR is not always the answer.

Some moments demand direct intervention, policy shifts, or public advocacy. Silence in the face of injustice isn't strategy—it's abdication.

The key is discernment. Ask:

- Will speaking up create defensiveness or momentum?
- Can the message travel faster through others than through me?
- Am I preserving trust or avoiding conflict?

Presence knows the difference.

REFLECTION:
What's Your Stealth Signature?

- Where have you shifted dynamics without being the center of the story?
- What methods of influence feel most natural to you—observation, storytelling, quiet alignment?

PRESENCE PRACTICE

This week, try the OSIE Model:

- Observe a dynamic that feels stuck.
- Seed a reframing insight.
- Influence through a trusted partner.
- Exit without needing credit.

Track the ripple.

ALIGNMENT CHALLENGE

Choose one systemic issue you've hesitated to confront directly. Map a stealth strategy:

- What insight can you introduce?
- Who might carry the message better than you?
- How will you know the shift is taking hold?

Remember: real leadership doesn't always come with a spotlight.

It comes with a shift in the system.

CHAPTER 9

Presence Under Pressure

It's easy to talk about presence when things are calm—when meetings are civil, plans are unfolding smoothly, and relationships are intact.

But real presence is forged in the fire.

It shows up when the conversation turns tense.

When decisions carry weight.

When your values are tested.

In those moments, you don't rise to the occasion. You fall back on your level of preparation, and your depth of presence.

The Pressure Paradox

Pressure doesn't change who you are. It reveals who you've been practicing to be.

This is where many HR professionals find themselves conflicted.

- Should I speak up, or stay neutral?
- Do I push back, or stay politically safe?
- Will I be seen as disruptive, or as principled?

These are not theoretical questions. They show up in boardrooms, performance reviews, restructures, and public-facing crises.

In these moments, presence is not about being calm. It's about being anchored—to your role, your voice, and your values.

A Moment That Defined My Shift

During a strategic leadership meeting, a high-ranking executive dismissed a workforce concern I raised. "That's not a priority right now," he said, brushing it off.

I felt the room contract. All eyes shifted. The easier choice would have been to let it go.

Instead, I paused. Took a breath. And said: "I understand it's not urgent on paper, but it is quietly impacting retention. If we wait for it to become a priority, we'll have fewer people left to serve the mission."

I didn't raise my voice. I didn't take offense. I stayed grounded, and I stayed in the conversation.

What I said wasn't radical, but it was honest. And afterward, several leaders said the same thing: "That needed to be said." It reminded me that when presence meets pressure, people remember how you made the room feel safer, smarter, and more strategic.

The Anatomy of Presence Under Pressure

When the heat rises, here's what real presence looks like:

- Centered body language—Shoulders relaxed. Voice steady. Eyes engaged.
- Clarity over emotion—You don't suppress emotion but you don't lead with it, either.
- Courage to interrupt—When necessary, you create a pause: "Can we slow down for a moment?" . . . "Can we check alignment before we decide?"
- Principled stance—You stay rooted in your values, even if it means standing alone.

This is not about perfection. It's about preparation.

Preparation Makes Presence Possible

You don't wait for pressure to build presence. You build it before the pressure arrives.

That means:

- Knowing your triggers—what causes you to shut down or overcompensate
- Practicing your grounding statements—phrases that reset tone or reframe tension
- Rehearsing high-integrity boundaries—how you'll respond if a line is crossed

Presence under pressure is less about the moment, and more about your readiness for it.

REFLECTION:
What Anchors You?

- When was the last time you felt under pressure but still showed up fully?
- What centering habits help you stay aligned in tense situations?
- Who do you become when you're not grounded?

PRESENCE PRACTICE

Before your next high-stakes meeting:

- Name your intention in writing:
  "I want to be a leader who..."
- Practice two grounding statements:
  "Let's pause to clarify what we're solving for."
  "Can I offer a different lens on this?"

After the meeting, debrief with a trusted peer, ask: "Did I show up in alignment with who I want to be?"

ALIGNMENT CHALLENGE

Think of a recent conversation where pressure pulled you out of alignment.

Revisit that moment:

- What would you do differently now?
- What practice might have helped you stay grounded?

Now, identify an upcoming moment of potential tension, and set an intention for how you will show up with presence under pressure.

Presence under pressure isn't about perfection. It's about precision of purpose. It's not how still you stand, but how deeply you stay rooted in what matters most. When tension rises, presence isn't just noticed—it's needed. And when it's grounded in trust, clarity, and courage, your presence doesn't just steady the room—it shifts it. Presence isn't proven in easy moments; it's forged in hard ones. In Part IV, we'll look at how to turn presence into a strategic advantage—one that accelerates decisions, strengthens culture, and positions you as an indispensable voice in the business.

Presence as Strategy

Up to this point, we've explored presence as something cultivated within: a mindset to model, a behavior to practice, and a way of engaging that transforms how others experience us. But presence isn't meant to stay internal. When fully developed, it becomes an accelerant—fueling influence, driving alignment, and shaping culture at scale.

This is where presence moves from personal power to strategic force.

In Part IV, we examine how presence becomes a lever for business impact. We move from individual rooms to enterprise rhythms—from conversations to culture shifts. Strategic presence allows HR leaders to not only sense what's happening in the organization but also steer it.

These chapters will explore how presence enables:

- Listening not just to gather feedback, but also to forecast risk and detect patterns.
- Being felt in ways that shift the emotional climate of leadership and unlock team performance.
- Reclaiming HR's identity—not as an internal service, but as a strategic function that drives sustainable growth.

Presence, when practiced with purpose, becomes more than a personal differentiator—it becomes a leadership multiplier.

Let's explore how.

CHAPTER 10

Leading Through Listening

*"After months of tension, I just listened—really
listened. The CFO pulled me aside and said, 'You
helped us move forward.' I didn't solve the issue.
I held space. And it made a difference."*
—HR Business Partner

There's a common myth in leadership: that influence is about speaking well.

But the most effective leaders I've worked with—the ones who command respect, build followership, and shift culture—don't just talk better.

They listen differently.

And when HR professionals build presence through listening, we do more than gather feedback.

We uncover truths.

We sense what others miss.

We create the conditions for trust.

From Transaction to Transformation: Two Ways HR Listens

Not all listening is created equal.

In HR, we're often taught to listen for resolution—to gather facts, mediate conflict, or close out a case. That's **transactional listening**: focused on efficiency, completion, and risk reduction.

But strategic HR leaders practice **transformational listening**. It's not about solving—it's about sensing. They listen to understand the deeper patterns shaping behavior, culture, and performance. And they use that insight to lead.

Transactional Listening	Transformational Listening
"Tell me what happened."	"What's this really about?"
Gathers facts for documentation	Surfaces insight to guide decisions
Focused on closing a case	Focused on uncovering patterns
Often reactive	Always proactive
Example: Exit interviews	Example: Stay conversations, team sensing

One gathers answers. The other **generates alignment**.

Listening as Leadership

Strategic listening is not passive. It's not waiting your turn or nodding politely.

It's active sensing:

- Listening for meaning, not just to words
- Noticing what's said, and what isn't
- Interpreting tone, energy, and timing as data
- Asking questions that unlock new insights

In fast-moving organizations, this kind of listening is rare. And that's what makes it powerful.

Because when leaders feel heard—not handled—your influence grows.

And when employees feel heard—not surveyed—engagement deepens.

The Hidden ROI of Listening

When you build listening into your presence, you:

- Catch misalignments early
- Detect culture erosion before the metrics show it
- Create psychological safety by modeling curiosity over judgment
- Shift your role from responder to sense-maker

Listening is presence in action. It tells the organization, "I'm paying attention, and I'm here to help make meaning."

A Listening Challenge for HR Leaders
Ask yourself:

- Do I listen to respond or to reflect?
- Do I make room for pauses or rush to fill them?
- When someone finishes speaking, do I follow with curiosity or conclusion?

Try this in your next one-on-one or team meeting:

1. Ask: "What's one thing you're thinking but haven't said yet?"
2. Let the silence hang. Then wait. That's where insight lives.

REFLECTION:
How Deeply Do You Listen?

- Who are the voices in your organization that go unheard most often?
- Where might you be listening more for compliance than connection?
- What would shift if your listening were part of your leadership strategy?

PRESENCE PRACTICE

Pick one recurring meeting this week. Your role: active listener.

- Say less.
- Ask more.
- Write down what's not being said, and what it might mean.
- After the meeting, reflect: What themes emerged? Where's the opportunity?

ALIGNMENT CHALLENGE

Design one process in your HR function—whether it's onboarding, exit interviews, or leadership check-ins—with listening as the anchor.

- What if exit interviews were about insight, not data collection?
- What if onboarding asked, "What energizes you?" instead of "What are your goals?"

Presence as strategy begins with listening as leadership. But not just any listening.

It's the kind of listening that slows down the noise and tunes into what matters. It hears the hesitations between words, the patterns beneath complaints, and the energy behind the unspoken. It's the leadership move that doesn't ask for the spotlight but earns influence because it builds trust in the dark.

When HR leaders listen this way, they stop reacting to issues, and start revealing what the business needs before anyone else can name it. They become not just responsive partners, but anticipatory ones.

Because in a world full of noise, the quietest presence often holds the greatest power.

And it starts with listening like it's your superpower—because it is.

CHAPTER 11

The Art of Being Felt, Not Just Heard

We've all been in meetings where someone says all the "right" things, but nothing lands. And we've also been in rooms where a single sentence from a grounded leader changes the entire energy.

That's the difference between being heard and being felt.

Words can inform.

But presence—true presence—transforms.

Strategic HR leaders understand this: It's not just about the message. It's about the imprint you leave.

What It Means to Be Felt

Being felt means your presence lingers:

- After the conversation ends, people reflect on what you said.

- In rooms you're not in, your perspective is referenced.
- When decisions are made, your framing shapes how others think.

This isn't about ego or theatrics. It's about emotional clarity, energetic grounding, and intentional communication that connects.

It's Not Charisma, It's Congruence

The leaders who are most felt aren't always the loudest. They're the ones who:

- Speak from alignment, not performance.
- Choose words with care—not to impress, but to illuminate.
- Express conviction without dismissing others' views.
- Show up consistently, especially under pressure.

When your energy and your message align, people experience trust, and that's what's remembered.

From HR as Function to HR as Force

As HR professionals, we're often expected to "soften" business decisions or clean up the impact of choices we weren't part of.

But when we lead from felt presence, we:

- Influence how decisions are made, not just how they're rolled out
- Shift meetings from transactional updates to transformational dialogue

- Elevate people strategy without needing the spotlight

This is what it means to be a force—not of resistance or control, but of clarity, credibility, and connection. A force that steadies the room. That names what others overlook. That makes complexity more navigable because your presence brings structure, not noise.

You become the person others seek out when things get hard—not because you have all the answers, but because they feel more grounded in your presence.

A Personal Reflection

I once coached a group session where a senior leader broke down in tears. Not from criticism but because someone in the group finally gave voice to their unspoken pressure and acknowledged the toll it was taking on them. I hadn't planned it. I had simply said: "You've been carrying a lot quietly, haven't you?"

In that moment, I wasn't performing a role. I was present, and they felt it.

That brief exchange shifted something—not just for the leader, but for the team watching. It gave permission for real emotion, honest reflection, and renewed trust.

That conversation shifted how they led their team for the rest of the year.

Being felt is a strategic act. It moves people toward courage, clarity, and connection.

REFLECTION:
Where Are You Being Remembered?

Think of a time when your presence changed a conversation. What made it impactful?
Where might you be delivering content, but not making contact?

PRESENCE PRACTICE

This week, ask yourself before each important interaction:

- Am I speaking from alignment or urgency?
- What emotion am I carrying into the room, and is it intentional?
- What do I want people to feel after this conversation?

Pause before you speak. Then choose clarity over commentary. Silence over filler. Curiosity over certainty.

ALIGNMENT CHALLENGE

Identify a message—whether it's about change, conflict, or culture—that you've been delivering from the head. Rewrite it from the heart.
Then share it in a way that allows space for others to respond—not just react.

When presence is felt, people don't just remember your words—they remember the shift you created in the room. That's influence at its most human and at its most powerful.

The next step is learning to channel that influence beyond moments of connection, into the structures, strategies, and culture of the business itself.

CHAPTER 12

Reclaiming the HR Identity

*"Someone once told me, 'You're not strategic—
you're in HR.' Now? I sit in budget meetings,
influence M&A decisions, and coach senior
leaders. We are not 'just HR.' We are architects
of the culture."*
—VP, People and Culture

HR has long wrestled with perception.

Are we policy police? People-pleasers? Culture cheerleaders? Or compliance enforcers?

We've been described as a support function, a cost center, a necessary burden. We've heard the jokes, absorbed the dismissals, and too often internalized the doubt.

But here's the truth: HR is not broken. It's just been boxed in.

And reclaiming the HR identity isn't about fixing ourselves.

It's about realigning the profession with its original—and future—power:

- To lead through people.
- To architect cultures.
- To unlock performance through presence.

The Old Story vs. the Real Work

The old story says that HR:

- Delivers training and handles terminations.
- Keeps leaders out of legal trouble.
- Steps in when "people problems" get messy.

But the real work of HR? It's enterprise leadership:

- Anticipating capability needs before strategy outpaces talent.
- Coaching leaders toward emotional maturity and team resilience.
- Aligning values, behaviors, and business outcomes.
- Creating cultures where high performance and well-being coexist.

The problem isn't that HR lacks value. It's that we've been trying to prove our value in systems that were never designed to understand it.

When Presence Reclaims the Narrative

When HR professionals lead with presence, everything shifts:

- We stop asking for permission to lead and start modeling what leadership looks like.
- We stop trying to prove our value through visibility and start embodying our value through influence.
- We stop defining ourselves by the "what" (programs, policies, plans) and start defining ourselves by the "how" (connection, clarity, cultural impact).

Presence isn't the opposite of performance.

It's the pathway back to purpose.

What Reclaiming Looks Like

Reclaiming the HR identity doesn't require a title change. It requires a posture change.

It means:

- Speaking the language of the business and the language of people.
- Holding both compassion and accountability in the same conversation.
- Walking into rooms not as support, but as a strategic equal.
- Refusing to shrink or harden based on others' discomfort with our clarity.

It also means being visible about the invisible work we do—naming our wins, capturing our insights, and helping organizations see that how people are treated is a strategy.

REFLECTION:
What Identity Have You Outgrown?

- What old HR narratives are you still carrying?
- Where have you been playing small to fit into a limited role?
- How do you define the HR profession now—in your own words?

PRESENCE PRACTICE

This week, reintroduce yourself.
Not your title. Your value.
Try:

- "I help leaders align people and performance to strategy."
- "My role is to translate between culture and capability."
- "I don't just manage talent—I architect trust and transformation."

Notice how others respond. Notice how you feel.

ALIGNMENT CHALLENGE

Audit your calendar and commitments:

- Where are you spending time reinforcing the old HR model?
- What would it look like to reallocate time to the work that truly drives culture, leadership, and performance?

Make one bold shift this month that reflects the HR identity you're reclaiming. Because presence isn't just about how others see you. It's about how you see yourself, and who you choose to be.

Your Presence Is the Proof

You don't need to convince anyone of your worth.

You need to lead in a way that reflects it.

Let your presence be your calling card.

Let your clarity be your credibility.

Let your consistency reclaim the narrative.

You are not "just HR."

You are the architect of how people experience work.

You are a strategist of systems, behavior, and belief.

You are the presence that helps others lead better.

It's time we stop asking to be invited to the table, and start anchoring it.

CHAPTER 13

Presence Across the Function

"In our HR cross-functional team meetings, our role is to ensure our business partners have the insights and tools they need to drive the organization's people strategy. We are the architects; our business partners are the builders. Together, we create a blueprint for a culture that works."
— VP, Compensation, Benefits & HRIS

When HR is at its best, presence isn't confined to a single role—it's woven through the entire function. It's the way each discipline—compensation, HRIS, talent acquisition, learning and development, employee relations—contributes to a seamless, credible employee experience.

This book has been written from the lens of the HR Business Partner because that's often where presence is most visible in the organization. But that visibility is built on the expertise, precision, and insight of every HR specialty. A compensation analyst who connects pay strategy to retention, an HRIS leader who ensures leaders have the right data at the right time, an L&D strategist who develops the skills the business will need tomorrow, a recruiter who identifies the talent to make it all happen—each is part of the same presence.

Presence across the function is about moving in concert—different skills, shared intention—so that every HR touchpoint strengthens the organization's strategy and culture.

The Collective Influence of HR

Let's name it: HR is a system of interdependent disciplines. We succeed not because one team shines, but because the entire ecosystem is aligned.

- Compensation and Benefits translate workforce strategy into tangible value. They ensure people are seen, rewarded, and retained.
- HRIS and Analytics make sense of complexity. They allow us to forecast, track, and pivot with data-informed precision.
- Talent Acquisition is often the first expression of organizational presence—how we recruit signals how we value.
- Learning and Development fuels the evolution of the workforce. They transform feedback into growth, and aspiration into capability.

These functions may operate behind the scenes, but their presence is felt every day—in the systems employees navigate, the benefits they count on, the training they receive, and the recognition they experience.

From Siloed Support to Strategic Symbiosis

Too often, we unintentionally silo our influence. The recruiter becomes "just" a gatekeeper. The L&D leader becomes "just" a trainer. The comp team becomes "just" a compliance check.

But when presence is practiced across the function, we stop being "just" anything. We start being just right for the strategic moment.

This requires:

- Shared language: so insights translate across teams
- Mutual respect: so no function is minimized
- Integrated rhythm: so we respond as one, not as parts

Presence isn't about visibility for one. It's about credibility for all.

Aligning Function with Purpose

Presence across the function means we align not just around tasks, but around impact. We center a unified purpose: to advance the employee experience in service of the business.

It means:

- We don't just respond to workforce needs—we shape them.
- We don't just collect data—we use it to forecast and influence.
- We don't just build programs—we build capacity.

When every HR function understands its stake in the employee value proposition, presence becomes amplified. We stop competing for attention and start compounding our impact.

REFLECTION:
Where Does Presence Live?

- Do we treat some HR roles as more "strategic" than others?
- How are we reinforcing the value of presence in every function?

ALIGNMENT CHALLENGE

Gather representatives from across the HR function. Ask:

- "What's one way our function shows presence—without needing a spotlight?"

Capture their responses. Then ask:

- "How can we intentionally elevate that presence across our internal partnerships?"

Presence is not a posture. It's a practice.

And when practiced across the HR function, presence becomes a culture.

Not just how HR shows up, but how the business experiences its people leaders.

This is how we move from function to force.

EPILOGUE

The Ongoing Work
of Presence

Presence is not a milestone you cross; it's a practice you return to—moment by moment, conversation by conversation.

It's in the choices you make when pressure rises.

It's in the questions you ask when clarity is needed.

It's in the quiet conviction that your influence is measured not by how often you speak, but by the weight of your words when you do.

Throughout this book, we've explored presence from many angles—inner and outer, individual and collective, personal and organizational. You've seen it as self-awareness in action, as listening that transforms, and as the connective tissue across every function of HR.

But presence is not reserved for the HR business partner, the executive table, or moments of high stakes. It belongs in the everyday rhythms of how we work—whether we're designing a compensation plan, onboarding a new hire, troubleshooting a system issue, or facilitating a leadership retreat.

When presence is cultivated across the function, HR stops being seen as a series of disconnected specialties and starts being experienced as a unified force—one that strengthens the employee experience and advances the organization's goals.

Your influence will rarely be about titles or spotlights. It will be about how you align your insight with your actions, your values with your voice, and your expertise with the moment at hand.

The true power of presence is not in being seen, but in aligning who you are with the change you lead.

A Message from Daphne

I'm Daphne B. Latimore, an organizational strategist, executive thought partner, and author of the leadership trilogy: The Power of Presence, Human Capital at the Core, and You Should Be a Coach.

Over the course of my career, I've moved from HR generalist to business partner to senior leader—always working shoulder-to-shoulder with specialists in HRIS, talent acquisition, compensation, benefits, and learning and development. I've navigated the realities of day-to-day operations, steered organizations through change, and contributed to boardroom decisions where people strategy shaped business outcomes.

Those experiences taught me this: presence is not a performance. It's a strategic imperative. It's how we influence decisions, shape culture, and elevate people—often without the spotlight.

Today, as Managing Partner of DB Latimore Professional Services Group, I partner with leaders and organizations to align culture with strategy, strengthen leadership behaviors, and unlock the full potential of their workforce.

This book was born from the quiet moments I've witnessed in HR leaders—moments when they became the steady voice in uncertainty, the bridge between perspectives, or the one who named what no one else could.

If The Power of Presence resonates with you—if you've ever been the person people seek out for clarity, connection, or courage—I'd love to keep the conversation going.

Let's explore how we can:

- Elevate HR as a strategic presence across the business
- Develop internal capacity through coaching-based leadership
- Align people strategy with business impact
- Build cultures where presence is practiced, not just expected

You can reach me at:
https://www.dblatimore.com

Or connect with me on LinkedIn:
https://www.linkedin.com/in/daphneblatimore

Because presence is how we turn HR from a function into a force.

Appendix
Certification Alignment Guides

How This Book Can Support Strategic HR Development

While not affiliated with or endorsed by SHRM or HRCI, *The Power of Presence* aligns with many of the core competencies and knowledge areas emphasized in their HR certification models.

The guides below are intended to help certified professionals reflect on how this book's themes and practices may support their continued growth and recertification efforts.

Whether you're a CHRO, an HR business partner, or a people leader navigating complexity, the content of this book encourages the leadership behaviors, mindset shifts, and enterprise thinking foundational to strategic HR.

Some Ways to Use These Guides

Use the suggested alignments to support:

- Recertification logs, using the Reflections
- Group coaching, lunch-and-learns, or internal workshops
- Peer discussions, using the Presence Practice exercises
- Mapping your personal growth against the competencies of strategic HR leadership

SHRM Behavioral Competency Alignments (Suggested)

Book Chapters	SHRM Competencies	Application
Part I (Chapters 1–3), "Understanding Presence"	Leadership and Navigation Communication	Enhances authenticity, influence, and interpersonal leadership presence
Chapter 2, "The Anatomy of HR Presence"	Relationship Management Emotional Intelligence	Builds awareness of how quiet leadership drives trust and connection
Chapter 3, "Credibility Before Visibility"	Business Acumen Consultation	Links presence to observable behaviors tied to organizational performance
Part II (Chapters 4–6), "The Strategic Shift"	Critical Evaluation Consultation HR Expertise	Guides leaders in aligning presence with enterprise-wide impact
Chapter 7, "Model the Mindset Before the Message"	Emotional Intelligence Ethical Practice	Reinforces intentional communication and composure before speaking or leading

Book Chapters	SHRM Competencies	Application
Chapter 8, "Leading in the Margins: The Art of Stealth HR"	Communication Relationship Management	Models subtle influence techniques and empowering leadership behaviors
Chapter 9, "Presence Under Pressure"	Resilience Communication	Provides tools for staying grounded and effective in crisis or high stress
Chapter 10, "Leading Through Listening"	Communication Relationship Management	Encourages feedback-rich cultures and psychologically safe environments
Chapter 11, "The Art of Being Felt, Not Just Heard"	Emotional Intelligence Leadership and Navigation	Promotes presence that translates into long-term impact and followership
Chapter 12, "Reclaiming the HR Identity"	Global and Cultural Effectiveness HR Expertise	Reinforces the strategic role of HR and redefines its influence in culture

HRCI Knowledge Area Alignments (Suggested)

Book Chapters	HRCI Functional Areas	Competency Focus
All chapters	Leadership and Strategy Talent Development	Develops core leadership presence, communication, and talent influence skills
Chapter 3, "Credibility Before Visibility" *and* Chapter 6, "Showing Up in the Rooms That Matter"	Employee and Labor Relations	Encourages behavioral accountability and psychological safety
Chapter 4, "From Policy to Pattern Recognition" *and* Chapter 5, "The Language of Influence"	Organizational Development Business Strategy	Aligns HR presence with long-term cultural and structural planning

Book Chapters	HRCI Functional Areas	Competency Focus
Chapter 9, "Presence Under Pressure"	Risk Management Crisis Communication	Applies composure to conflict, risk, and high-stakes decision-making
Chapter 11, "The Art of Being Felt, Not Just Heard"	Talent Development Leadership Coaching	Fosters peer and team coaching mindset to grow presence in others
Chapter 12, "Reclaiming the HR Identity"	Change Management Organizational Effectiveness	Encourages adaptable leadership presence through continuous change